GROWING ORCHIDS MADE SIMPLE

How to care for your
orchids from start to finish

KAELEY GREENE

Table of Contents

CHAPTER 1

Orchids: How to Grow Them

Orchid flowers are among the most beautiful, complex, and diverse in the plant kingdom. Over 30,000 different species and at least 200,000 hybrids make up the largest family of flowering plants on the planet. It doesn't matter if you live in the tropics or the arctic. Orchids can be found anywhere. As a result of the orchid's remarkable ability to adapt to its surroundings, there is a wide range of orchid species. As a result of the wide variety of orchid species that can be grown in a wide range of environments, finding one that will thrive in your home or office, whether it be a kitchen window or an entire greenhouse, is not difficult.

Tropics are home to the majority of the world's cultivated orchids. They attach themselves to trees and other plants in their natural habitat. Roots that are thick and white are well-suited to absorbing water and nutrients. These orchids, which grow in the trees rather than on the ground, are accustomed to good air circulation and plenty of light because they are used to this environment. All year round, they prefer a 12-hour day and a high level of light intensity, which is comparable to the conditions of midsummer in temperate regions.

Is it difficult to grow orchids?

Many of them are Even professional growers have

difficulty keeping some plants alive, much less bringing them into bloom. Many varieties of orchids, as well as hundreds of hybrids, thrive in a sunny window or under artificial lighting.

Begin by selecting a less fussy variety that is suited to the growing conditions you can provide. A mature plant is easier to please than a young one, so go for the most expensive option you can find that's still in bloom.

Generally speaking, orchids can be divided into two broad categories based on how they grow. The leaves of monopodial orchids are arranged in opposition to one another along the stem of the plant. It is from these leaves that the flower stem emerges. These orchids include the phalaenopsis and vandas.

Growth occurs in a sympodial pattern, which is the most common. The old rhizome of these orchids sends out new shoots, allowing them to spread horizontally. At the top of the new shoots, leaves and flower scapes begin to grow. Swollen shoots known as pseudobulbs form in many sympodial orchid species to help the plant withstand prolonged periods of dryness. Cattleya, cymbidium, oncidium, and dendrobium are all sympodial orchids.

To further narrow down your search, consider the temperature, humidity, and light levels preferred by the orchids in their native habitat. In the humid tropics, orchids like phalaenopsis and paphiopedilum prefer temperatures between 73°F and 85°F, with humidity levels between 80 percent and 90%. They prefer an east or southeast window that isn't too bright.

Temperatures between 55 and 70 degrees Fahrenheit are ideal for orchids like cymbidiums and dendrobiums, which require a steady supply of moisture and good air circulation. Generally speaking, they prefer a south-facing window, but they may require some shade in the hottest months.

Cattleyas and some oncidiums thrive in climates with short, cool days. Temperatures of 80 to 90 degrees Fahrenheit can be tolerated for a long period of time, followed by a distinct rainy period. They require a lot of light, so they should be placed near a window that faces south.

The cloud forests are home to orchids like masdevallia and epidendrum, which thrive in temperatures ranging from 60 to 70 degrees Fahrenheit and high humidity levels. Filtered light is ideal for these orchids, as it isn't too bright.

To look after ornithological plants

You cannot give general care and cultivation instructions for 30,000 different species of orchids. However, an orchid's appearance can reveal its needs for light, water, and growing media.

Most cattleya and oncidium plants require a high-light environment if they have few or leathery leaves. Light-sensitive plants, like some phalaenopsis and most paphiopedilum, should not be placed in a sunny south-facing window because their leaves are soft and limp.

It should be watered sparingly and grown on chunks of bark or lava rock if the pseudobulbs are large. It may be necessary to water the orchid more frequently if it doesn't have pseudobulbs, or to use a growing medium that retains moisture better, such as sphagnum moss.

CHAPTER 2

Light

As a general rule, orchids require a lot of light. In order to get the best results, they should be exposed to 12 to 14 hours of sunlight every day, year-round. The length of day and the intensity of natural light do not vary as much in a tropical climate as they do in a temperate one. It's possible to keep your orchids happy during the winter months by moving them around and supplementing with artificial light.

In general, orchids do best in rooms with windows that face south or east. Windows facing west or north tend to be hotter and darker. Your orchids will thrive under artificial lighting even if you don't have a good window location. If you're using four-foot fluorescent bulbs, keep your orchids no more than six to eight inches away from the bulbs' base. When it comes to the relative merits of using cool white, warm white, or even grow light bulbs, there is no consensus. For the most part, the new full-spectrum bulbs are the best option. Vandas and cymbidiums, orchids with high light requirements, may require high-intensity discharge lighting in order to blossom. Read Growing Under Lights for more information.

The ever-expanding media landscape

Paphiopedilums and some cymbidiums, for example, are terrestrial orchids that grow in soil. Tropical orchids, on the other hand, are almost exclusively epiphytes, meaning that they grow in the air rather than on the ground. Velamen, a layer of white cells that acts as a sponge, covers the roots of these plants. The coating also acts as a heat and moisture barrier for the roots.

A good orchid growing medium must be able to quickly drain water and allow for good air circulation. It must also provide a safe place for the roots to attach themselves to. They can thrive in a variety of substrates depending on the type of orchid. Tree ferns and cork can also be used to support some epiphytic orchids. Nuggets of fir bark are the most commonly used growing medium.

Watering

Watering

Drought is more tolerable for orchids than excessive moisture for the most part. Allowing an orchid to sit in a waterlogged pot will quickly kill it. The plant will suffocate and die if it doesn't get enough air.

Orchids should be watered once a week at the most. Excess water should not come into contact with the roots or the growing medium, and the growing medium should be allowed to dry between waterings. Most orchids take several months to get back to full growth after being re-potted. During this period of adjustment, use water sparingly.

Humidity

Humidity levels of 60% to 80% are ideal for most tropical orchids. There are a number of ways that orchid growers keep their plants happy in the winter, including using humidifiers and placing them in trays of gravel or rubber grids that are set in waterproof containers. Misting orchids can also be beneficial in some cases.

Fertilizer

There are very few nutrients in orchid growing mediums, so orchids must be fertilized in order to thrive. Dilute a liquid fertilizer more than you would for other plants when using it on a lawn or garden lawn. When plants are actively growing, fertilizer should be applied. Most orchids should not be fertilized during the winter months or immediately after a re-potting. While 30-10-10 fertilizer is popular, some growers prefer 10-10-10 or even 10-10-30 as an alternative. Using fish emulsion or seaweed extracts to mist your orchids will give them micronutrients.

Re-Potting and Potting Up

In general, orchids thrive in a small pot. You can easily remove the roots or cut apart the plastic pots when you need to re-pot your plants. Foam "peanuts" can be used to fill the bottom of the pot and help with drainage. Fill the pot with fir bark chunks or other growing medium as you hang the orchid above it. The plant's crown should be slightly lower than the top of the pot's rim. While the roots are establishing themselves, it may be necessary to secure the plant with some wire.

Some orchids require yearly repotting. Other people may be content to stay in the same pot for seven or more years. Re-potting your orchid should only be done when absolutely necessary. Disturbing orchids makes them angry. The growing medium should be re-potted if it has begun to break down to the point where aeration has been reduced, if the roots have extended beyond the pot, or if new growth has thrown the plant's equilibrium off.

Propagation

It is extremely difficult to grow orchids from seed. Orchid seeds, in contrast to those of other plants, lack nutritional storage tissues. There must be a specific fungus that can penetrate the seed's root system and convert nutrients into something the plant can use in order for it to grow. A seed capsule of orchid usually releases millions of microscopic seeds, which can travel hundreds of miles from the mother plant, in order to overcome the obstacles.

Working in sterile conditions is necessary for orchid seed propagation. A gelatinous substance containing nutrients and growth hormones must be used to grow the seeds. You'll also need to be a patient person. First leaves don't appear for months, and they're only noticeable with a magnifying glass. After that, the roots appear. A flower will not appear for at least three years, and possibly up to eight years.

It is much easier to grow orchids through division than through seed germination. However, it's important to keep in mind that dividing a plant means a year or more of no blooms. In addition, as the orchid grows in size, it produces more flowers. When it comes to small divisions, it can take decades for them to reach a mature state.

CHAPTER 3

Other than plants and animals, orchids are capable of producing hybrids within and across genera. This allows for a mind-boggling number of hybrids, which is why orchids have such complicated names.

Most orchids bloom once a year, but they may bloom more frequently when they are in a happy mood. • It's best to buy an orchid when it's in bloom if you want one that only blooms during a specific time of year.

When an orchid blooms, it typically lasts between six and ten weeks.

When orchids are re-potted, they typically don't flower for at least a year. Consider purchasing your orchids as potted plants rather than as bareroots if you can.

Orchids for Beginners: Easy Varieties

— Cattleya: 55 to 90 degrees F; 40 to 80 percent humidity;

alternate wet and dry; coarse fir bark.

Temperatures between 65 and 85 degrees Fahrenheit and humidity levels between 40 and 70 percent are ideal for Phalaenopsis.

High-intensity lighting, temperatures ranging from 40 to 60 percent humidity, and a bark or fluffy moss mix are recommended for the Paphiopedilum.

THE END